539.7

J. C. T.

MILESTONES
IN MODERN SCIENCE

SPLITTING THE
ATOM

Alan Morton

Evans

Published by Evans Brothers Limited
2A Portman Mansions
Chiltern Street
London W1U 6NR

First published 2005

British Library Cataloguing in Publication Data

Morton, Alan
Splitting the atom. - (Milestones in modern science)
  1. Atomic theory – Juvenile literature
  2. Nuclear physics – Juvenile literature
  3. Discoveries in science - Juvenile literature
  I. Title
539'7

ISBN 0237527367

Consultant: Dr Anne Whitehead
Editor: Sonya Newland
Designer: D.R. Ink, info@d-r-ink.com
Picture researcher: Julia Bird

Acknowledgements

Cover Los Alamos National Laboratory/Science Photo Library; Science Photo Library; CERN/Science Photo Library 3 EFDA-JET/Science Photo Library 4(t) US Department of Energy/Science Photo Library 4(b) Laguna Design/Science Photo Library 5 Fermilab/Science Photo Library 6 © Archivo Iconografico, S.A./Corbis 7(tl) Robert Walster/Big Blu Ltd 7(bl) Robert Walster/Big Blu Ltd 7(br) © Royalty-Free/Corbis 8(t) © Stefano Blanchetti/Corbis 8(b) Science Photo Library 9(t) Sheila Terry/Science Photo Library 10 Martyn F. Chillmaid/Science Photo Library 11(t) Science Museum/Science & Society Picture Library 11(b) Dept. of Physics, Imperial College/Science Photo Library 12(t) Science Photo Library 12(b) Science Photo Library 13 © Bettmann/Corbis 14 Science Photo Library 15(t) Sheila Terry/Science Photo Library 15(b) Jean-Loup Charmet/Science Photo Library 16(b) Martin Dohrn/Science Photo Library 17 National Museum of Photography, Film & Television/Science & Society Picture Library 19(t) Science Photo Library 20 Science Museum/Science & Society Picture Library 21 Science Photo Library 22 Science Museum/Science & Society Picture Library 23(t) Mehau Kulyik/Science Photo Library 23(b) Lande Collection/American Institute of Physics/Science Photo Library 24(t) C. Powell, P. Fowler and D. Perkins/Science Photo Library 25(b) David Parker/Science Photo Library 26 Lawrence Berkeley Laboratory/Science Photo Library 27(t) Science Photo Library 27(b) Los Alamos National Laboratory/Science Photo Library 28 © Corbis 29(t) Science Museum/Science & Society Picture Library 29(b) Lawrence Berkeley Laboratory/Science Photo Library 30(t) Argonne National Laboratory/Science Photo Library 30(b) Argonne National Laboratory/Science Photo Library 31 © Corbis 32(b) © Corbis 33(background) Los Alamos Laboratory/Science Photo Library 33(inset) USAir Force/Science Source/Science Photo Library 34 NASA/Science Photo Library 35(b) EFDA-JET/Science Photo Library 36 Los Alamos Laboratory/Science Photo Library 37(t) Martin Bond/Science Photo Library 37(b) © Bettmann/Corbis 38 CERN/Science Photo Library 39 David Parker/Science Photo Library 40 Fermilab/Science Photo Library 41 CERN/Science & Society Picture Library 42 Photo © Estate of Francis Bello/Science Photo Library 43 ArSciMed/Science Photo Library 44 Laguna Design/Science Photo Library

CONTENTS

'The atomic bomb embodies the results of a combination of genius and patience as remarkable as any in the history of mankind.'

WRITER AND PHILOSOPHER BERTRAND RUSSELL, 1945

Introduction

ABOVE: *Atomic bombs work by releasing energy in the form of heat and radiation from the nucleus of atoms. Such weapons are the result of a century of investigating and harnessing the properties of atoms.*

BELOW: *This computer artwork represents a hydrogen atom – the simplest and most widespread element in the Universe. The pink sphere at the centre is the proton; the wavy lines represent the path of the electron.*

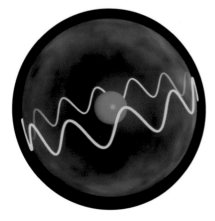

Atoms make up all matter – ourselves and everything around us; they are the building blocks of our Universe. The idea of these fundamental particles was first suggested by the ancient Greeks, but at the time no one could actually prove they existed, so the theory of atoms was quickly overtaken by other explanations of the structure of matter. Thousands of years passed, and it was not until the end of the eighteenth century that atomic theory was revived.

When scientists returned to the idea of the atom, they were faced with many questions. How could they prove atoms existed? Were atoms solid? If not, what existed inside them? How did they stick together to build up everything we see around us? At times it seemed as though the more they found out, the more there was to discover!

At first, scientists thought that atoms were the smallest particles that could exist, but towards the end of the nineteenth century, even smaller particles were found inside the atom – protons, neutrons and electrons. Once they knew this, scientists could begin to work

out how atoms interacted with one another. This knowledge opened up a whole new field of scientific study – subatomic physics. Understanding the basic properties of the atom led to the discovery of new chemical elements, radioactivity and much more. But there were still greater possibilities hidden inside the atom. In 1938, a team of physicists working in Berlin succeeded in splitting the nucleus of a uranium atom. In the process, they noticed that energy was released; if this energy could be controlled, it could be used to make weapons more powerful than anyone had previously imagined possible. With the Second World War looming, the race to harness nuclear energy began.

Knowledge about the atom does not only have scientific implications; it also has very practical applications. We exploit properties of the atom in everything from electricity supply to mobile phones, from genetics to medicine, from nuclear weapons to space flight. Without knowledge of the internal workings of the atom, there would be no modern industrial society. All this happened in a remarkably short space of time. In 1900 atomic research was only important for a few scientists working on it. By 1945, after the United States dropped the first atomic bombs on the Japanese cities of Hiroshima and Nagasaki, almost everyone realised that subatomic physics had changed the world – and there could be no going back. The story of how the atom was split is a fascinating tale of competition and cooperation, of human ingenuity and imagination; it is truly one of the most dramatic tales in scientific history.

CHAPTER ONE

'*Material objects are of two kinds, atoms and compounds of atoms. The atoms themselves cannot be swamped by any force, for they are preserved indefinitely by their absolute solidity.*'

ROMAN PHILOSOPHER LUCRETIUS (C. 99–C. 55 BC)

Understanding Atoms

ALTHOUGH UNDERSTANDING ATOMS HAS BEEN A RELATIVELY RECENT phenomenon, the idea of tiny particles making up everything around us was first suggested many centuries ago, in the time of the ancient Greeks. Despite this, it was not until the beginning of the nineteenth century that scientists began to unravel the mysteries of the atom.

ABOVE: *The Greek philosopher Democritus, who first suggested that all matter was made up of atoms – tiny, indivisible particles.*

ANCIENT IDEAS ABOUT THE ATOM

As far back as the fifth century BC, philosophers had speculated about the structure of matter and questioned whether everything in the Universe could be made up of tiny particles – units that were so small they could not be divided up any further. The word *atomos* was used to describe these units, and means 'uncuttable' in ancient Greek.

One of the first people to suggest what we now think of as the modern theory of the atom was the Greek philosopher Democritus (*c.* 470–*c.* 400 BC). Although he did not conduct experiments, or even make observations or mathematical deductions, he came up with several very modern-sounding scientific ideas. One of these was that all matter was made up of solid

ABOVE/LEFT: *The four elements (clockwise from top left): water, fire, earth and air. Aristotle believed that combinations of these elements made up all matter; he was considered to be a greater philosopher than Democritus so his theory of matter was accepted and atomic theory was forgotten.*

particles that were indivisible; nothing smaller could exist. These particles were so tiny they could not be seen by the human eye. Not all his suggestions about atoms were correct, but they were certainly quite close to the mark.

Unfortunately, there was no way of proving or disproving this theory – people either believed it or they didn't. One of the most famous of the ancient Greeks to disagree with Democritus was the great philosopher Aristotle (384–322 BC). Aristotle claimed that a smallest part of matter did not exist, and that all substances were made up of four elements: water, fire, air and earth. People chose to believe Aristotle's view of the structure of matter, and the idea of the atom was not seriously considered by scientists again until the eighteenth century, when new evidence for their existence was discovered.

CHEMICAL ELEMENTS

In 1789, the French chemist Antoine Lavoisier (1743–94) drew up a table of what he called chemical 'elements'. These elements were substances such as carbon, gold or oxygen, which could not be broken down into simpler substances. Lavoisier identified 33 elements and put them in categories according to their properties: gases, non-metals, metals and earths. There are other chemicals called compounds, which are different combinations of the basic elements. Not all the elements Lavoisier identified appear on the periodic table we are familiar with today. Some of them were what we now call oxides, and can in fact be divided by chemical reactions. However, Lavoisier's table was the first time anyone had attempted to classify substances. It paved the way for other scientists to start investigating the elements further.

The English scientist John Dalton was the first person since ancient times to suggest an 'atomic' theory of what the elements were made from, in 1803. Unlike Democritus, he based his theory on evidence he had gathered by conducting experiments on the chemical elements. Dalton stated that all matter was made of atoms, which he pictured as tiny billiard balls,

ABOVE: *Antoine Lavoisier drew up a table of chemical elements – the first time anyone had attempted to classify substances, and the forerunner of the periodic table we use today.*

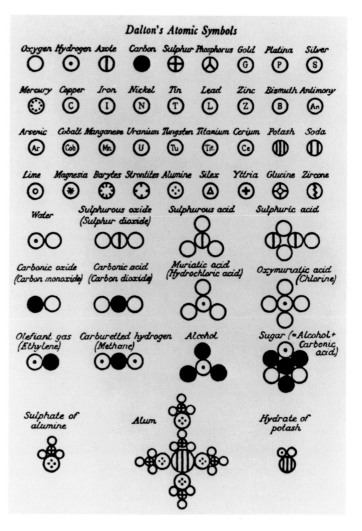

RIGHT: *John Dalton's table of atomic symbols. We now know that some of these are incorrect – water is not HO, for example – but Dalton's ideas about chemical reactions and atoms started other scientists thinking about atomic theories.*

Key People

John Dalton (1766–1844) was an English scientist and teacher. He was fascinated by all types of scientific study, and made some important observations about the weather, including what caused rain. His studies of gases led to what we now call Dalton's Law, which states that the total pressure exerted by a mixture of gases equals the sum of the pressures of the individual gases in the mixture. It was his theory of atoms, however, that made him most famous. He thought that all atoms of the same element had the same weight, but atoms of different elements had different weights. He created a table of chemical elements based on their 'atomic weights'. The modern periodic table uses atomic mass (a measure of matter) as a way of categorising elements.

Fact

THE IMPORTANCE OF ELECTRICITY

Electricity was a new phenomenon in the early nineteenth century, but scientists quickly harnessed it to use in experiments. This resulted in the discovery of new chemical elements, and a greater understanding of the ones that scientists already knew about. The scientist and inventor Humphry Davy (1778–1829) discovered that if he passed an electric current through some substances, they decomposed (this process is now called electrolysis). When Davy passed an electric current through some compounds he found they separated into their different components. In this way, Davy discovered the elements potassium and sodium, amongst others. When an electric current is passed through water, it splits the water down into the elements hydrogen and oxygen, always in the proportions 2:1. This led scientists to speculate that the basic unit of an element was the atom, and that all the atoms of a particular element had identical properties.

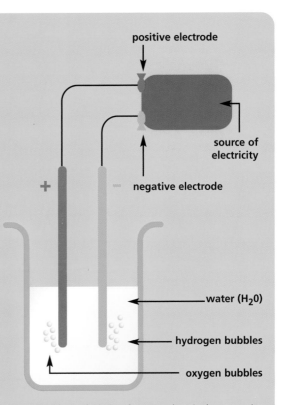

positive electrode

source of electricity

negative electrode

water (H_2O)

hydrogen bubbles

oxygen bubbles

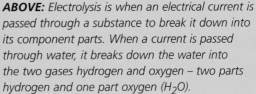

ABOVE: *Electrolysis is when an electrical current is passed through a substance to break it down into its component parts. When a current is passed through water, it breaks down the water into the two gases hydrogen and oxygen – two parts hydrogen and one part oxygen (H_2O).*

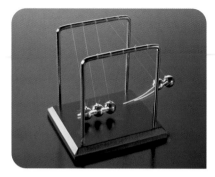

ABOVE: *The transfer of energy can be seen in the working of 'Newton's Cradle'. As the balls swing, the kinetic energy (energy of motion) is transferred from one ball to another until the ball at the other end moves upwards. It will reach a point where it can swing no higher and its kinetic energy becomes potential energy (energy of position). As it drops back down, the energy is once more converted to kinetic energy.*

and which were indivisible and indestructible. These atoms were different in each of the elements, and he believed that, for example, an atom of gold was made of solid gold.

From this time onwards, scientists began to take the atomic theory of matter more seriously. In 1815, another English scientist and doctor, William Prout (1785–1850), suggested that perhaps all atoms were simply different arrangements of an even more fundamental 'building block'. He named this unit the 'protyle'. Prout thought that a protyle might be like the lightest atom, hydrogen. Different atoms would simply be groups of the same protyle, but in different combinations. Imagine a building site; the same kind of bricks can be used to build a house, a factory, a railway station, depending on how the bricks are arranged. In the same way, different arrangements of protyles would make the different kinds of atoms. Prout's idea of a basic building block turned out to be very influential on later atomic theories – although not quite as he expected.

ATOMS AND ENERGY

By the middle of the nineteenth century, many scientists were convinced that physical and chemical phenomena such as heat, light, electricity and motion, were just different forms of energy that could be converted from one to another. For example, James Joule (1818–89) conducted an experiment in which he turned a wheel immersed in a liquid. Some of the kinetic energy (the energy an object has because of its motion) from the movement of the wheel was converted into heat. The temperature of the water increased as a result. In this experiment, kinetic energy had been turned into thermal energy. It helped the scientists understand these processes if they thought of atoms as having a definite size. They imagined them to be spheres that were around 10^{-10} metres in diameter. A million atoms would make up the thickness of a sheet of paper.

LEFT: Dmitri Mendeleev was one of the first scientists to reorganise the table of elements so they appeared in groups sharing similar properties; these groups were called periods.

Fact

ATOMIC SPECTRA

An important clue to the internal structure of atoms was discovered when heating chemicals until they glowed. Scientists noticed that if sodium was present in the chemical, for example, the glow had a characteristic orange colour (you can see this in sodium street lights). Using a glass prism to split up the light into its different colours, chemists mapped the colours of light from each element. These patterns of light, called spectra, were unique for each element. From this evidence they concluded that all the atoms of one element must have the same internal structure.

ABOVE: This is the spectrum of colours from the element helium. Every element has its own unique colour spectrum – a kind of finger-print that allows scientists to determine the presence of these elements in particular substances.

There were still many questions. As they learnt more about the various forms of energy and the different elements that made up compounds, scientists realised that the atoms in a substance must be held together by some kind of force. However, because atoms are so small it was very difficult to discover exactly what this force was and how it worked.

As more elements were discovered, two scientists – the Englishman John Newlands (1837–98) and the Russian chemist Dmitri Mendeleev (1834–1907) – independently drew up a new type of table of chemical elements. They arranged the different elements in periods – groups of elements that had similar chemical properties. Similar elements such as lithium, sodium and potassium, all fell in one column in his table. This suggested that the atoms of all the different elements in one column or group had structural features in common. But what were these features?

CHAPTER TWO

'Could anything at first sight seem more impractical than a body which is so small that its mass is an insignificant fraction of the mass of an atom of hydrogen?' **PHYSICIST J. J. THOMSON ON THE ELECTRON, 1934**

What's Inside the Atom?

ABOVE: *The first human X-ray, made by Wilhelm Röntgen, showing his wife's hand (wearing a ring). He won the Nobel Prize in 1901 for his discovery of X-rays.*

BELOW: *Röntgen's X-ray machine looks very simple by today's standards. The generator (B) supplied electricity to the cathode-ray tube (T). This generated X-rays, which left an image of the hand on a covered photographic plate (C).*

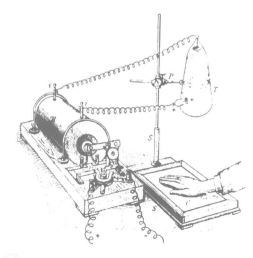

AT THE BEGINNING OF THE TWENTIETH century science and technology were developing rapidly. Many people saw the results of this in their everyday lives – electric lights replaced oil lamps, cars replaced horse-drawn carriages. There were also breakthroughs in understanding atoms, and these were built on several key discoveries made at the end of the nineteenth century.

THE DISCOVERY OF X-RAYS

Finding out about X-rays was the first key development that helped scientists on their way to understanding the atom. X-rays were discovered by the German scientist Wilhelm Röntgen (1845–1923). During experiments, he noticed a phenomenon that no one had seen before – it could darken photographic plates even when they were wrapped in black paper. Röntgen named the phenomenon X-rays because it was so mysterious. Since X-rays could pass through solid objects, doctors were soon using them to examine broken bones.

X-rays also gave information about atoms, because they are caused by the movement of electrons (the negatively charged particles that move around the nucleus of atoms). In 1913, after the electron had been discovered and explained (see p. 14–16), the scientist Henry Moseley (1887–1915) conducted several experiments with X-rays which revealed that the atomic number in the periodic table represented the positive charge in the atom. Using a cathode-ray tube, he bombarded different metals with streams of high-energy electrons. He noticed that each of the metals emitted X-rays with different wavelengths. The cathode rays were knocking out the innermost electrons from the atoms in the metal; this was causing electrons in the outer shells to fall into the inner shell and this process caused X-rays to be emitted. The amount of energy needed to knock out an electron from the inner shell of an atom depends on the number of protons in the nucleus. This meant that by measuring the frequency of X-rays emitted by outer electrons falling into the inner shell, scientists could work out the number of protons in the nucleus and the positive charge of an atom.

THE DISCOVERY OF RADIOACTIVITY

Finding one type of radiation, X-rays, prompted a frantic hunt for others. In France in 1896, Henri Becquerel (1852–1908) sorted through a collection of mineral specimens to find the ones that affected photographic plates. He discovered several specimens that blackened the plates in a similar way to X-rays. These mineral samples contained the element uranium, the heaviest element then known. Becquerel realised that uranium naturally emitted a type of radiation, invisible to the human eye. This form of radiation became known as radioactivity.

After Becquerel had discovered it, other scientists jumped on the bandwagon and began to study its

RIGHT: *Henri Becquerel, who discovered radioactivity in uranium.*

Fact

RADIOACTIVITY

When Henri Becquerel and Marie Curie first discovered radio-activity, they did not realise how unusual it was. It was only later that scientists learned of its special properties. Atoms in radioactive elements like uranium are unstable; they emit particles or rays – this is radiation. There are three types of radioactive radiation: alpha particles, beta particles and gamma rays. When alpha or beta particles are emitted, an element can change, or 'decay' into atoms of a different element. The third type of radioactive decay, involving gamma rays, does not change an element.

ABOVE: *This photograph led to the discovery of radioactivity in 1896. The dark patches show where Henri Becquerel placed crystals of uranium salt on a photographic plate.*

properties in more detail. The Polish-born physicist Marie Curie (1867–1934) was the most famous of these. She obtained large amounts of uranium ore and began to purify it. It was painstaking work but she was rewarded when, even after removing all the uranium from the ore, there were still signs of radioactivity being emitted. She concluded that there must be other elements in the ore that were radioactive. Curie finally separated small quantities of two previously unidentified elements – radium and polonium.

Both these elements were found to be useful in hospitals for the treatment of cancer, as their radiation could be used to kill cancerous cells. But the new elements also helped scientists to uncover the next clues about the structure of the atom.

DISCOVERING THE ELECTRON

By the 1890s the main use for electricity was for lighting buildings. The new electricity supply companies were in fierce competition with established companies supplying oil or coal-gas for lighting. The first electric light bulbs were dim, short-lived, and costly. They were equivalent to a modern 25-watt bulb and using them was 1,000 times more expensive! Making better light bulbs was a high priority.

Electric lighting works by passing an electric current through a metal filament in the light bulb. The filament glows brightly. The glass bulb has to be a vacuum – it must have no air in it at all – or the filament will burn out too quickly.

Radio 'valves' were similar to light bulbs; they used metal filaments in glass bulbs. Radio valves amplified the weak radio signals that were picked up by an aerial so people

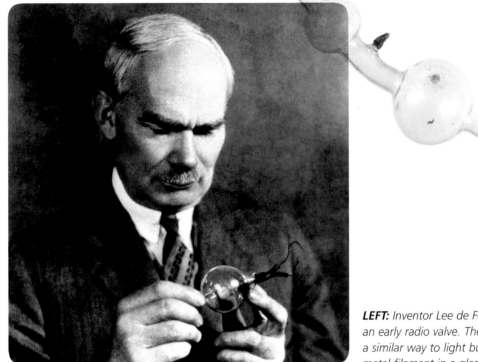

LEFT: *Inventor Lee de Forest, holding an early radio valve. These worked in a similar way to light bulbs, using a metal filament in a glass bulb.*

could hear the transmitted signal using headphones or a loudspeaker. Valves are the bulky and power-guzzling ancestors of the transistors and integrated circuits we use today.

In the 1890s many scientists and engineers studied the behaviour of electric currents through wires in glass tubes, hoping to make better lighting and radios. One puzzle they encountered was the behaviour of electric currents passing through a glass tube that had no air at all inside (a vacuum tube). Where the beam of electricity hit the end wall of the tube, there was a glowing spot on the glass. The rays that caused this effect were called cathode rays because they originated from the cathode, or negative electrode. These glass tubes are the forerunners of all conventional television and computer screens, which are still called cathode ray tubes, or CRTs.

But what exactly were cathode rays? The debate raged about whether they were particles or waves. Working in Cambridge, England in 1897, the physicist J. J. Thomson (1856–1940) finally found the answer.

BELOW: *This type of cathode-ray tube is called a 'Crookes tube'. British physicist Sir William Crookes used these from around 1878 to investigate cathode rays. Crookes' experiments led J. J. Thomson to discover that cathode rays were actually beams of electrons.*

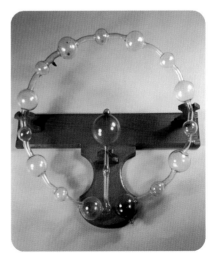

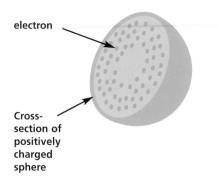

electron

Cross-section of positively charged sphere

ABOVE: *From his discovery of the negatively charged particle, Thomson worked out a model of the atom that became known as the 'plum-pudding' model. This atom was a solid sphere, with electrons dotted around inside it like currants inside a plum pudding.*

In his experiments he found he was able to change the direction of a beam of cathode rays using both magnetic and electric fields. Thomson's experiments proved that cathode rays were particles with a negative electric charge. He also suggested their mass was only 1/2000 that of a hydrogen atom.

He called his new particle the 'corpuscle', but the name didn't catch on and it was renamed the 'electron'. The unit of negative charge was the first subatomic particle to be discovered.

The discovery of the electron raised even more questions. Electrons are negatively charged. Atoms are electrically neutral. This meant that inside the atom there must be a positive charge that cancelled out the negative charge. What was it? And what other secrets did atoms have locked away?

FINDING THE NUCLEUS

Encouraged by these discoveries, physicists tried new experiments. They noticed that atoms of polonium –

Fact

ELECTRONS – WAVES OR PARTICLES?

J. J. Thomson was certain that the electron was a particle because it behaved in the same way as other particles. As quantum mechanics (the study of physical phenomena on the tiniest scales) developed in the 1920s, it became clear that electrons could also behave like waves. For example, they could produce interference patterns like those made by beams of light. In 1927 G. P. Thomson (J. J. Thomson's son) showed the wave properties of the electron.

ABOVE: *Light behaves like a wave, because it produces interference patterns like these. If you drop pebbles in still water near each other, the waves that are caused move outwards in increasing circles. The waves caused by one pebble will eventually meet and interfere with the waves of the other pebbles.*

Fact

THE PHOTOELECTRIC EFFECT

In the first few years of the twentieth century scientists were coming up with all sorts of theories about the nature of processes they observed in chemistry and physics. One of the most important of these was the explanation of what we call the photoelectric effect, by Albert Einstein (1879-1955) in 1905.

Einstein noticed that when light falls on a metal plate, it can make electrons jump out of it. What puzzled him was that this did not work with all forms of light. Einstein realised that the light hit the metal in a series of 'packets' that he called quanta. The energy of these quanta depended on the colour of the light: blue or ultraviolet light had high energy, but red had low energy. Only packets with a certain level of energy could be absorbed by the atom and cause it to eject an electron. Einstein's theory of the photoelectric effect made other scientists think about the idea of packets of light.

The photoelectric effect is still important today, in devices like televisions and video cameras. It is used to convert light from a picture into electrical signals, which can then be recorded or broadcast. It was also used to explain how light stimulates the production of glucose in green plants. The photoelectric effect is the starting point for all food chains.

RIGHT: Albert Einstein was awarded the Nobel Prize for his explanation of the photoelectric effect.

one of the elements discovered by Marie Curie – self-destruct. This process is called radioactive decay. In radioactive decay, the atoms disintegrate, firing off a large chunk (an alpha particle). Alpha particles were the ideal probes to find more information about the structure of the atom. Alpha particles were later proved to be helium atoms minus their electrons.

In Manchester Hans Geiger (1882–1945) and Ernest Marsden (1889–1970) conducted an experiment in which they aimed these alpha particles at gold foil – extremely thin sheets of gold. Most alpha particles passed straight through the gold foil, but unexpectedly a very small number hit the foil and bounced back. Geiger and Marsden could not explain why.

BELOW: When alpha particles were fired at a thin sheet of gold foil, most of them passed straight through. However, if the positively charged alpha particle directly hit the nucleus of one of the gold atoms, the positive charge in the nucleus repelled the particle and bounced it back.

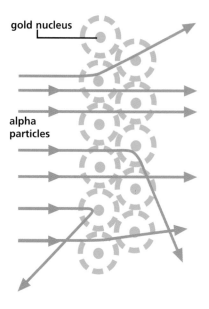

gold nucleus

alpha particles

BELOW: In Rutherford's model of the atom, the electrons orbited the nucleus. To keep the negatively charged electrons in orbit, the nucleus had to have a positive electric charge. It also contained over 99.9 per cent of the atom's mass.

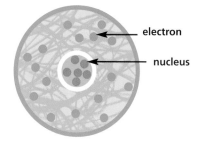

electron

nucleus

In 1911, the English physicist Ernest Rutherford hit on the explanation for this. The atoms in the gold foil must be largely made up of empty space, so most of the alpha particles passed straight through the foil. The interesting phenomenon was that a few of the particles bounced back as if they had hit something solid. Rutherford suggested that at the centre of each of the atoms was a core, or nucleus. He believed this was only about 1/10,000 the diameter of the atom, but thought the nucleus contained most of the mass of the atom as well as the positive charge that scientists had been looking for. Because alpha particles are positively charged, if they collided with the nucleus of an atom in the gold foil, the positive charges would repel each other and the alpha particle would bounce back. Rutherford compared the collision between the alpha particle and the nucleus to a battleship firing a shell at a sheet of tissue paper, and the shell rebounding!

THE PLANETARY MODEL OF THE ATOM

A Danish scientist, Niels Bohr (1885–1962), took the next step. Two years after Rutherford explained his theory of the atom, Bohr came up with a different model, based on the same idea. He agreed that the electrons orbited the nucleus, but he suggested that these orbits took the form of a number of fixed 'shells', with the electrons moving around in them. This became known as the planetary model of the atom. A shell, or orbit, could contain one or two electrons whizzing around. Bohr said that electrons in the orbits closest to the nucleus had less energy than those in orbits further away. While it stayed in a particular orbit, the energy of the electron was fixed. When an electron moved closer to the nucleus into a lower energy orbit, it emitted the excess energy as a flash of light.

This explained why atomic spectra consisted of particular colours – specific frequencies of light. Those precise frequencies – and only those – could appear (disappear) when an electron moved from one orbit or energy level to another.

Key People

Ernest Rutherford (1871–1937) was one of the most talented physicists of the early twentieth century. He was awarded the Nobel Prize in 1908 for his work on radioactivity. From this he moved on to studying the nature of the atom, and in 1911 he explained the famous gold-foil experiment, which showed that there was a positively charged nucleus at the centre of an atom. He was made director of the famous Cavendish Laboratory in Cambridge (a post previously held by J. J. Thomson) in 1919. During his time there he made many contributions to physics, including researching nuclear reactions. Rutherford did not believe the energy produced in these reactions could ever be harnessed by scientists, but this turned out to be his greatest mistake. His work helped pave the way for the discovery of nuclear fission (see p. 29) and the development of nuclear weapons.

BELOW: Bohr's atomic model had electrons moving round the nucleus in orbits or 'shells', in much the same way as the planets in our Solar System move around the Sun, so it became known as the planetary model. It was not quite complete, but it was closer than scientists had been before to an accurate understanding of atomic structure.

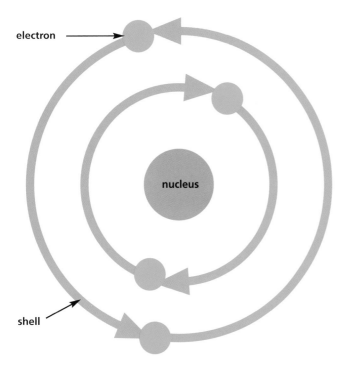

electron

nucleus

shell

Fact

ELECTRON SHELLS
Today we know that each electron shell can hold only a certain number of electrons. The first shell (the one closest to the nucleus) cannot hold more than two electrons. The second shell can hold up to eight electrons. The third can hold 18. The maximum number of shells in an atom is seven; the seventh shell can theoretically hold up to 98 electrons.

Fact

MASS AND WEIGHT

★ Mass is a measure of how much matter something contains.

★ Weight is a measure of how strongly gravity pulls on matter.

Imagine you were an astronaut. If you travelled to the Moon, your weight would change because the pull of gravity is much weaker there than on Earth. Your mass would stay the same, though, because your body would still be made up of the same amount of matter.

PROVING THE EXISTENCE OF THE PROTON

Scientists now knew that the nucleus had a positive electric charge, but they still didn't know what caused it. Did the negatively charged electrons have positively charged counterparts? If so, where were they? Another English scientist, Francis Aston (1877–1945), took a step towards answering this question. He was working on experiments that would 'weigh' atoms very precisely, and he managed to measure the masses of neon atoms. He thought that all atoms of the same element would have the same mass, but to his surprise he found two different measurements of mass in neon atoms. There are actually two different varieties, or isotopes, of neon. One isotope is 20 times, the other 22 times the mass of hydrogen. Aston went on to invent a device called a mass spectrograph, which allowed him to separate the isotopes of different elements. He applied this invention to other chemical elements and discovered many other isotopes – 212 in all. In 1922, Aston was awarded the Nobel Prize for his work.

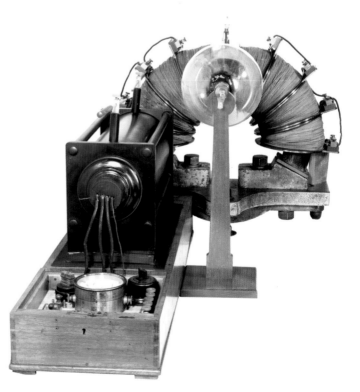

RIGHT: Aston's mass spectrograph could separate isotopes of various elements. The globe contained a compound of the substance being tested; an electric current was passed through it, which knocked electrons from the atoms.

Rutherford was interested in Aston's discovery of isotopes, and it made him think of William Prout's theory of protyles. Perhaps the hydrogen nucleus was a building block of all nuclei after all. Rutherford suggested the name 'proton' for this unit.

In 1925, a young research student at the Cavendish Laboratory in Cambridge, England, named Patrick Blackett (1897–1974), provided further evidence for the existence of the proton in the nucleus of an atom. He successfully photographed a collision between an alpha particle and a nitrogen nucleus. What emerged from the collision was a proton – a positively charged particle that had come from the nitrogen nucleus.

ABOVE: *Blackett's photograph, showing alpha particles scattering from atomic nuclei of different masses. Here, the alpha particles stream upwards through the cloud chamber; one of them scatters a proton through the water vapour that fills the chamber. The proton shoots upwards (this is the fainter track moving to the left from the bottom right). The alpha particle, which is heavier, is slightly deflected to the right.*

Fact

CLOUD CHAMBERS AND GEIGER COUNTERS

Atoms are so small that they are impossible to see even with the best optical microscopes. In the early twentieth century new methods were devised to detect subatomic particles. When he photographed the collision between the alpha particle and the nitrogen nucleus, Blackett used one of these new methods – the cloud chamber. This was a cylinder filled with water vapour. When an electrically charged particle passed through the chamber some of the electrons were knocked off the atoms and water droplets formed on them. A trail of droplets traced the track of the particle through the cloud chamber. These could be photographed and analysed.

It was difficult to count large numbers of particles using a cloud chamber. Early versions of the Geiger-Muller counter did that. These detected the charged particle as it entered the counter tube and triggered an electric current. The current passed between the outer metal tube and a central wire along the axis of the tube. Counting the spurts of current measured the number of particles passing through the counter.

29, 1932

A NEW RAY

DR. CHADWICK'S SEARCH FOR " NEUTRONS "

Dr. James Chadwick, F.R.S., Fellow of Gonville and Caius College, Cambridge, in an interview on Saturday said that the result of his experiments in search of the particles called " neutrons " had not, at the moment, led to anything definite, and the element of doubt about the discovery still existed.

There was, however, a distinct possibility that investigations were proceeding along the right lines. In that case a definite conclusion might be arrived at in a few days, and on the other hand it might be months. Dr. Chadwick described his experiments as the normal and logical conclusion of the investigations of Lord Rutherford 10 years ago. Positive results in the search for " neutrons " would add considerably to the existing knowledge on the subject of the construction of matter, and as such would be of the greatest interest to science, but, to humanity in general the ultimate success or otherwise of the experiments that were being carried out in this direction would make no difference.

Lord Rutherford, at the conclusion of his lecture at the Royal Institution on Saturday, confirmed in a statement to a representative of *The Times* the importance of the experiments by Dr. Chadwick. They seemed to point, he said, to the existence of a ray whose particles, known as " neutrons," were indifferent to the strongest electrical and magnetic forces. He did not, however, confirm the assumption that these particles were matter in the everyday sense of the word from the fact that their collisions obeyed the laws of momentum ; nor the further assumption that they moved at a speed more than a tenth of that of light or electricity.

Lord Rutherford's own lecture dealt with the " Discovery and Properties of the Electron," and in the course of it he conducted a number of experiments in the generation of cathode rays, with glass tubes and bulbs used 50 or more years ago by Sir William Crookes, and with others lent by Sir William Pope.

The discovery in 1897, said Lord Rutherford, of the negative electron had been of profound significance to science. The electron tube was essential to-day not only for the generation of continuous radiations, but for their reception, and thus rendered possible the rapid development of radio-telephony and broadcasting. When they looked back, it became clear that the year 1895 marked what they might call the definite line between the old and the new physics. It was in that year that Röntgen made his famous discovery of the X-rays. The importance of the discovery was really, in a sense, greater than itself, because it gave the impetus to experiments which led to two epoch-marking discoveries, of radioactivity by Becquerel in 1896 and of the electron in 1897. Those two discoveries opened up new vistas of the wonderful ways in which Nature worked. They gave us, for the first time, methods for attacking the question of the structure of the atom, and we now had a fairly definite general view of that structure; and they had given us, for the first time, a fairly clear idea of the mechanism of radiation.

ABOVE: *In 1932, the world was told of Chadwick's discovery of the neutron – the particle that existed with protons in the nucleus of an atom.*

WHAT WERE THE MISSING PARTICLES?

There was still a missing link. In order for atoms to be neutral, the positive charge in the nucleus must equal the negative charge so that they cancel each other out. But experiments to measure the weight of the nuclei of atoms showed that there was a discrepancy. For example, the nucleus of a nitrogen atom weighs as much as 14 protons, but it only has seven electrons. How could the atom be electrically neutral if it had more protons than electrons? Because scientists at the time only knew about these two particles, some of them suggested that the atom must contain additional electrons, in the nucleus, which neutralised some of the extra proton charges. If this was the case, a nitrogen atom would have 14 protons and seven electrons in the nucleus, and a further seven electrons in the shells outside the nucleus.

Many scientists did not believe that extra electrons were the answer to the puzzle, though, and researchers in laboratories round the world took up the challenge of finding the missing part of the nucleus. The answer was discovered in 1932, once again in Cambridge, where James Chadwick was conducting experiments in which he bombarded atoms of beryllium with alpha particles. What he found was another constituent of the nucleus, a particle with the same mass as the proton but no electric charge. They called this the neutron. So nuclei contained protons and neutrons. Nitrogen actually had seven protons and seven neutrons in its nucleus.

Finally scientists had cracked the atom – they knew it contained protons, neutrons and electrons. As it turned out, though, this was just the beginning. Atomic structure was not at all simple – an atom of uranium, the heaviest known element, was a complex structure containing hundreds of protons and electrons. So, the research did not stop there. People began to find out more and more about the nature of atoms and what they could do.

LEFT: Beryllium – the element James Chadwick used in his experiments that revealed the neutron – has four electrons (seen orbiting in shells outside the nucleus). Inside the nucleus (the pink sphere in the middle), beryllium has four protons and, as Chadwick discovered, five neutrons.

Key People

James Chadwick (1891–1974) was an English physicist who found the missing piece of the puzzle of atomic structure when he proved the existence of the neutron – the particle in the nucleus of an atom with no electrical charge. Chadwick began his studies on particle behaviour under Ernest Rutherford at the Physical Laboratory in Manchester in 1911. He also spent some time working with Hans Geiger in Germany, but eventually returned to England, where he rejoined Rutherford, now working at the Cavendish Laboratory in Cambridge.

His breakthrough came in 1932, after he began experiments in which he bombarded atoms of elements with alpha particles. This revealed the long-sought-after neutral particle that explained the discrepancy between an element's atomic number and its atomic mass. Chadwick was awarded the Nobel Prize for Physics in 1935 and was knighted in 1945.

By using streams of particles in this way, Chadwick helped pave the way for developments in nuclear fission that occurred rapidly over the following decade and a half, culminating with the detonation of the first atomic bombs in 1945.

CHAPTER THREE

'If I could remember the names of all these particles, I'd be a botanist.' **PHYSICIST ENRICO FERMI**

Unlocking the Secrets of the Nucleus

AS THE TWENTIETH CENTURY PROGRESSED, NEW TECHNOLOGY BECAME available which allowed scientists to delve even deeper into the structure of the atom and to understand how the subatomic particles worked. Most importantly they wanted to crack open the nucleus. Once they knew how to do this, they could manipulate atomic structure. The study of the nucleus became known as nuclear physics, and it set scientists on the path to creating a form of power greater than anything mankind had ever known.

ABOVE: This is a coloured image showing the emission of radioactive alpha particles from the element radium.

ACCELERATORS AND COUNTERS

Up until around 1930, scientists had used radioactive materials such as radium or polonium to provide streams of fast-moving particles to bombard nuclei in order to find out more about how they worked. But these radioactive sources were difficult to prepare and very expensive, as well as being dangerous to use. Researchers wondered if there was an alternative substance that could provide the necessary particles in a more efficient way. They also began thinking about how to create a machine that could send a beam of particles travelling at high speeds to facilitate these experiments.

LEFT: *A modern particle accelerator, based on Cockcroft and Walton's original. This is used in the first stages of particle acceleration in the Fermi National Accelerator Laboratory (Fermilab) in Chicago, USA.*

Technology began to catch up with scientific theory around this time, mostly developed by the new electrical industries. This meant that researchers now had access to large magnets, transformers for producing high voltages of electricity, and pumps for removing air so it did not interfere with the accelerating particles. Now they had better equipment at their disposal, teams of physicists and engineers raced to build the first particle accelerator or 'atom smasher'.

The first working accelerator was built by John Cockcroft (1897–1967) and Ernest Walton (1903–95) in Cambridge. It could produce a flow of protons accelerated using 100,000 volts of electricity. Was that high enough to force protons into the nucleus of a target atom? Remarkably, it was.

It had been calculated earlier that alpha particles could 'leak' out of the nucleus. Cockcroft reasoned that if this was the case, it should be possible for protons to burrow back in. His theory proved correct. In 1932 Cockcroft and Walton became the first people to split the atom. Using protons as 'bullets' they shot them at lithium atoms and made the nuclei disintegrate.

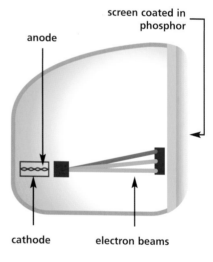

ABOVE: *In an ordinary television or computer screen, electrons are taken from the cathode and sped up. Electromagnets fixed in a vacuum change their direction and they are then smashed into the screen, which has a phosphor coating. The collision causes a 'pixel' of colour on the screen. Particle accelerators work in a similar way, except that the particles move much faster and the collision results in lots of subatomic particles.*

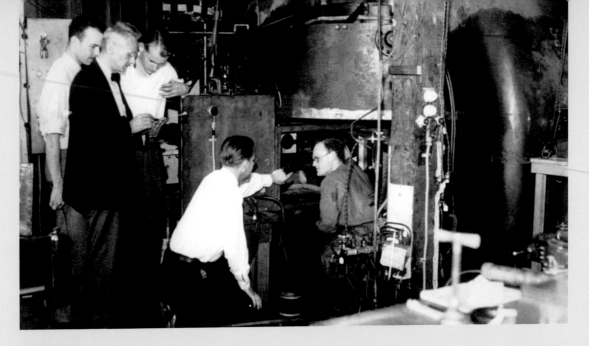

ABOVE: *Ernest Lawrence kneels in front of the cyclotron in 1932.*

Within weeks, Ernest Lawrence (1901–58) and Stanley Livingston (1905–86) in Berkeley, California had similar success. They called their particle accelerator the cyclotron. In this machine the particles travelled in circles, getting faster on each circuit. Today most of the large accelerators are based on a similar design to the cyclotron.

The work of Lawrence at the Radiation Laboratory in Berkeley paved the way for what became known as 'Big Physics' – experiments that involved large teams of physicists and engineers, huge laboratories and enormous budgets.

WHAT DID PARTICLE ACCELERATORS REVEAL?

Using particle accelerators for experiments in nuclear physics had one significant advantage. The kinetic energy (the energy an object has as a result of its motion) of the protons was known. Using protons with known energy to bombard nuclei in a target meant the energy involved in any nuclear reactions could be accurately calculated. For the first time, Einstein's famous equation linking energy and mass, $E = mc^2$, could be tested.

Using the latest technology, the German physicist Werner Heisenberg (1901–76) showed that there was a specific force, the strong interaction, holding the protons and neutrons in the nucleus. This force was in addition to the gravitational and electrical forces that scientists already knew about.

One big puzzle remained. In one type of radioactive decay, beta decay, an electron was emitted from the nucleus. Of course, to many scientists, this seemed to back up the idea that in fact electrons do exist in the nucleus, as they had believed before the existence of the neutron was revealed. As before, they thought these 'nuclear' electrons were in addition to the atomic electrons circulating in the outer reaches of the atom. However, this contradicted everything that recent research had revealed.

In 1934, Italian physicist Enrico Fermi suggested a new explanation for beta decay. He explained that at a point in the radioactive decay, a neutron actually changed into a proton. In the same instant, an electron was created. Fermi also suggested that in order to ensure energy was conserved, a neutral particle with very little mass was emitted alongside the electron. He called this particle the 'neutrino' (Italian for 'little neutral one') to distinguish it from the neutron.

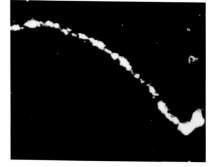

ABOVE: *A photograph of beta decay of a helium nucleus. The short, thick track at the bottom right is the nucleus, the curving track moving away from it is an electron, created during the process of decay.*

NUCLEAR FISSION

What other secrets remained locked inside the nucleus? Over the next few years scientists all over the

Key People

Enrico Fermi (1901–54) was an Italian physicist. His first great success came in 1934 when he solved the mystery of beta decay. He continued his work on radioactive elements and soon proved that the nucleus of almost any element could be transformed if it was bombarded with neutrons, rather than protons as had been used previously. His experiments with neutron bombardment led to the discovery of nuclear fission – a turning point in the history of understanding the atom. Fermi later became a US citizen, and Fermilab in Chicago is named after him. He was awarded the Nobel Prize for Physics in 1938.

Fact

$E=mc^2$

One of Einstein's greatest theories was that matter and energy are just different forms of the same thing. Matter can therefore be turned into energy and vice versa. In Einstein's famous equation $E=mc^2$, E is energy, m is mass and c is the speed of light squared. So, to find the energy, you multiply the mass by the speed of light squared. When a stream of neutrons collides with a nucleus, it forces some of the mass of that nucleus to be released. It is released in the form of energy. When scientists measured the energy released during experiments it confirmed Einstein's equation.

RIGHT: *Enrico Fermi and his team in Italy worked tirelessly to solve the Uranium Problem (see p. 29), but it was scientists in Germany who finally managed to split the atom.*

world tried to find out. They soon realised that instead of using protons, which are positively charged, as the 'smashers' in their experiments, it would be better to use neutrons. Unlike protons, these were not repelled by the positive electric charges in the nucleus when they got near it, and could therefore be much more effective.

Fermi pioneered this technique at his laboratory in Rome. His team found a way of producing a stream of neutrons and bombarded elements such as uranium with the particles. Through this process Fermi hoped to create a few atoms of some elements that did not occur naturally on Earth. These would be even heavier than uranium – the heaviest known naturally occurring chemical element.

In their attempt to create the first man-made, or 'artificial' elements, Fermi and his team tried many methods. They even used the goldfish pond in the grounds of their laboratory! Members of the team in Rome were rather confused by the results of their experiments with neutrons and uranium, though. They found that many different types of radioactivity were produced and they could not explain why. They called this the Uranium Problem.

News of the Uranium Problem reached two chemists working in Berlin, Otto Hahn (1879–1968) and Fritz Strassmann (1902–80). Together with Lise Meitner (1878–1968), they solved the problem in 1938. They realised that by bombarding uranium with neutrons, they actually caused the atom – or more specifically the nucleus – to split into smaller pieces, creating different radioactive elements. They had, quite literally, split the atom.

They named this process nuclear fission and pointed out that during the reaction huge amounts of energy could be released – much more than in other atomic or nuclear processes.

ABOVE: *Lise Meitner and Otto Hahn, whose experiments with neutron bombardment of the element uranium revealed that the nucleus of an atom could be split, creating other elements.*

Fact

ANTIMATTER

At around this time, the theoretical physicist Paul Dirac (1902-84) in Cambridge made a surprising prediction. He said that as well as matter there must be antimatter. What he meant by this was that the atoms and particles scientists at the time knew existed were in a state of positive energy, but there must also be negative energy. Dirac believed that for every particle that exists, there is an antiparticle. As particles are made up of matter, antiparticles are made of antimatter. They have exactly the same mass as the particle, but an opposite electric charge. Soon after Dirac's prediction, the American physicist Carl Anderson (1905-91) proved it to be true. He was studying cosmic rays – high-energy particles from outer space – and among them he found positive electrons, positrons. We now known that every particle has its antimatter equivalent.

ABOVE: *This shows the tracks of a pair of electrons (green) and their antiparticles, positrons (red). An electron is also displaced (the green track from top to bottom).*

CHAPTER FOUR

'The energy produced by the breaking down of the atom is a very poor kind of thing. Anyone who expects a source of power from the transformation of the atom is talking moonshine.'

PHYSICIST ERNEST RUTHERFORD, 1933

Fission Unleashed

ABOVE: Scientists in Chicago, Illinois, witness the first controlled nuclear chain reaction (in reactor, at right).

BELOW: A page from Fermi's patent for what he called the 'neutronic reactor'. It was based on the first nuclear pile, the blueprint for the nuclear reactors that would follow.

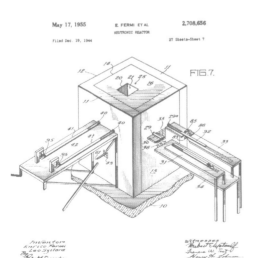

THE DISCOVERY OF FISSION IN THE WINTER of 1938–39 opened up a new path for nuclear scientists. If it could be harnessed and controlled, the energy released by the process of fission could be very powerful. As the Second World War loomed, physicists in several countries speculated that fission might be used to make a very powerful bomb.

SETTING OFF A CHAIN REACTION

When one nucleus of uranium is split, the energy released is the equivalent to that of a flea jumping. By itself the fission of one nucleus – one flea jump – was useless. The aim was to get more fleas to jump together, so that their combined energy could be used! In the process of fission, neutrons are released from the uranium. What intrigued physicists was the possibility that the neutrons released during one uranium fission could be made to make more uranium nuclei fission, with more neutrons released, and so on. This process is called a chain reaction, and huge amounts of energy could be released in this way.

If the chain reaction went slowly, the release of the energy would be steady and under control. As long as it was controlled, uranium could be used as a fuel in a reactor to produce heat for generating electricity – a nuclear power station. If the chain reaction went very fast, almost instantaneously, then the amount of energy released would be so great that it would cause a huge explosion – an atomic bomb.

The first problem nuclear physicists encountered was that only one isotope of uranium, uranium 235, was efficient enough to be used in nuclear fisson. Uranium 235 made up less than one per cent of uranium and the nuclei were too rare to be hit by passing neutrons. The rest, uranium 238, absorbed neutrons, so it would be very difficult, if not impossible, to set up a chain reaction from ordinary uranium. The physicists' initial excitement wore off.

THE ROAD TO NUCLEAR WEAPONS

The Second World War broke out in 1939. The Germans believed that the war would be over very quickly, so even if nuclear weapons were possible, they would not be developed in time to affect the outcome of the war. They saw nuclear research as a longer-term study – at least at the beginning of the war – and did not make it a high priority.

The British government, however, was worried that the Germans might develop a nuclear weapon. It gathered together its best physicists and invested a lot of money in finding a way of causing fission in ordinary uranium. Scientists in America were also trying the solve the problem.

In Britain two refugee physicists from Germany, Otto Frisch and Rudolf Peierls, realised that if they could separate the isotope uranium 235 from ordinary uranium, uranium 238, it would be possible to make a weapon from the isotope. This work led to the Tube Alloys project in Britain, which was later merged with the much larger Manhattan Project in the United States.

LEFT: The Los Alamos laboratory in New Mexico was the heart of the Manhattan Project, set up to develop atomic weapons using nuclear fission.

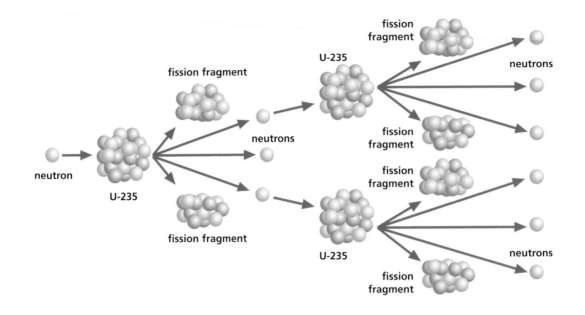

ABOVE: *In a nuclear chain reaction neutrons are fired at an element such as uranium 235. When the neutron collides with the uranium nucleus, it splits into fragments and releases other neutrons. In turn, these collide with more uranium nuclei, releasing more and more energy.*

The Manhattan Project pursued two lines of development to make atomic bombs. The first was to separate uranium 235. This was not easy, and could only be done by physical means – the fissionable isotope has to be physically separated from the majority of the more common uranium 238. The process was complicated, and had to be repeated many times to produce enough uranium 235 to be used in a weapon. Although they continued this line of investigation they also looked at other possibilities.

Key People

Otto Frisch (1904–79) and **Rudolf Peierls** (1907–95) were the two men who solved the problem of how to isolate enough uranium 235 to use in a nuclear weapon. Frisch was born in Austria and Peierls was German, but both men fled to England at the beginning of the Second World War and helped the British with their atomic research. They were both key members of the team brought together for the Manhattan Project in the USA. This project finally developed a successful atomic weapon. After the war, both men returned to England from America. Frisch worked at the famous Atomic Energy Research Establishment at Harwell. Peierls worked as Professor of Physics at Birmingham University and Oxford University.

The most promising of these was to create a completely new element that was fissionable. This was possible because if a chain reaction was set up in a nuclear reactor, some of the neutrons converted uranium 238 into plutonium 239, a fissionable material. The advantage of this method was that the plutonium could then be separated from the uranium by chemical methods.

In December 1942 Fermi and his colleagues built the first nuclear reactor (or pile) in Chicago and set off a nuclear reaction. Once they had proved that it worked, the reactor was dismantled and larger reactors were built for plutonium production at Hanford in Washington State.

The purified uranium 235 and the plutonium were incorporated into weapons at Los Alamos, New Mexico. The design of the new plutonium weapon was tested at Alamogordo, New Mexico in July 1945. It was successful. Now scientists could build bombs for real targets. Two atomic bombs were dropped on the Japanese cities of Hiroshima and Nagasaki in August the same year. Many thousands of people died, including American prisoners of war. Soon afterwards the Japanese capitulated and the war ended.

The sheer power of these bombs and the devastation they caused shocked the world. Just over 100 years after John Dalton had revived the atomic theory of matter, scientists had used the atom to create a weapon that could change the world.

ABOVE: *The devastation caused by the atomic bomb dropped on the Japanese city of Hiroshima at the end of the Second World War shocked the world. For the first time, people realised the terrifying power of nuclear weapons.*

BACKGROUND: *The atomic explosion after the detonation of the first atomic bomb during trials at Alamorgordo in July 1945.*

Fact

URANIUM ISOTOPES

All the atoms of uranium have 92 protons in the nucleus – this is what defines them as uranium. But uranium nuclei have different numbers of neutrons in them. The most common isotope, uranium 238, has 238 protons and neutrons altogether. That total includes 92 protons so the number of neutrons is 238 minus 92 = 146. The number of neutrons in uranium 235 is 235 less 92 = 143.

CHAPTER FIVE

'The unleashed power of the atom has changed everything save our modes of thinking and we thus drift toward unparalleled catastrophe.' **PHYSICIST ALBERT EINSTEIN, 1946**

A Nuclear Future?

AFTER THE SECOND WORLD WAR, SEVERAL COUNTRIES – INCLUDING Britain, Russia and China – set up programmes to develop nuclear weapons even further. Making plutonium required nuclear reactors. The heat from these reactors could be used to produce steam that in turn could be used to generate electricity. Gradually the designs of reactors built for military purposes were used for civil nuclear power stations.

ABOVE: *Nuclear fusion is a process that takes place naturally in the Sun, creating enough energy to keep it burning. Hydrogen nuclei are fused to create helium nuclei.*

NUCLEAR FUSION

Nuclear fusion works in the opposite way to fission. In this process, instead of being split in two, the nuclei of atoms are fused together. This mimics what happens in the Sun. Energy is released during nuclear fusion just as it is during nuclear fission. The machines built to cause nuclear fusion are called fusion reactors.

Scientists and engineers have tried to use deuterium, an isotope of hydrogen, in a fusion reactor. The technology required is very advanced and still has not been completed. The most promising design for a fusion reactor is the Tokamak, a doughnut-shaped device developed by the Russians.

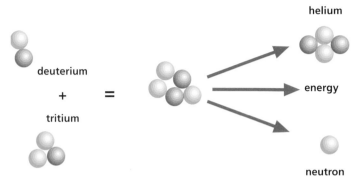

LEFT: In nuclear fusion, two hydrogen isotopes (in this case deuterium and tritium) are fused. In the process, energy is released in the form of a neutron. The reaction creates helium.

To achieve fusion, the deuterium needs to be in the form of a plasma, a state in which the nuclei have been stripped of their electrons. The plasma has to be heated to very high temperatures to allow fusion. For fusion to take place the plasma has to be kept away from the walls of the Tokamak, so it is confined by precisely shaped magnetic fields.

BELOW: This huge machine is the Joint European Torus (JET) at Oxfordshire in England. The ring-shaped chamber confines plasma that is used in fusion reactions. The machine was built so that scientists could investigate nuclear fusion and perhaps find ways of using it as a source of commercial power.

Building a reactor that produces more energy than it consumes has proved to be more difficult than many of the early supporters of fusion research expected. The most recent international project is JET (Joint European Torus), built in England. This has provided information that will be used to design a bigger and better machine, ITER (International Thermonuclear Experimental Reactor), that will take us one step closer to a design for a commercial fusion power station.

Fusion as a source of commercial power is still some decades away; however, if it can be made to work safely and efficiently, it will provide a fuel that is cheap and readily available. The machines themselves will be highly radioactive and will have to be maintained by robots rather than humans, but unlike nuclear power stations there will be no radioactive waste from the fuel.

BELOW: The explosion caused by the detonation of the first hydrogen (or thermonuclear) bomb in the South Pacific in 1952.

Fact

ELECTRICITY FROM NUCLEAR POWER

In Britain the first nuclear power station, Calder Hall, opened in 1956. This originally produced plutonium for weapons, but was soon supplying electricity for the National Grid. In the USA, a compact reactor designed for propelling submarines was developed, the Pressurised Water Reactor (PWR). This was first used to generate electricity on land at Shippingport, Pennsylvania.

RIGHT: *Nuclear power stations like this one in Switzerland are used to generate power for many different purposes – from creating the radioactive elements used in weapons, to generating electricity for commercial use.*

NUCLEAR WEAPONS

During the development of the atomic bomb based on the fission process, several scientists speculated that it might be possible to build an even more powerful weapon based on the fusion process. These weapons are called hydrogen bombs.

Hydrogen bombs are actually detonated by atomic (fission) bombs. This explosion creates the conditions for the fusion process to take place. Fusion weapons can be built to be much larger than fission weapons, and are much more destructive.

With the development of nuclear weapons in a number of states over the past few years, there have been negotiations to reduce the nuclear arsenals of states with nuclear weapons and to prevent the spread of weapons to non-nuclear states. These negotiations have had significant but limited success. One major concern about the spread of civilian nuclear power is that it gives states access to nuclear technology and know-how, some of which can be used to develop weapons as well as nuclear power.

BELOW: *This was the type of atomic bomb dropped on the Japanese city of Hiroshima in 1945. It is a fission bomb, nicknamed 'Little Boy'. Almost as soon as fission bombs were created, scientists began thinking of ways to produce even more powerful weapons using atomic processes. The result was a different kind of bomb that used the process of nuclear fusion.*

CHAPTER SIX

'The terror of the atom age is not the violence of the new power but the speed of man's adjustment to it – the speed of his acceptance.'
AMERICAN WRITER E. B. WHITE

Particle Physics Today

ABOVE: *The coloured tracks here are created by particles in a bubble chamber (see p. 39) after they have been subjected to a high-speed collision. The tracks created allow scientists to study the behaviour of the particles.*

THE APPARENT SIMPLICITY OF NUCLEAR physics in its early days came to an abrupt end. The model of the atom in which a cloud of electrons surrounded a nucleus consisting of protons and neutrons could not explain a spate of new discoveries: the positive electron, the neutrino, strange particles ... the list grew longer and longer.

TECHNOLOGY SINCE THE WAR

The model became complicated in the 1950s and 1960s when a new generation of accelerators was developed. These accelerators were much bigger and more powerful than those built before the war. In part this became possible because of new technologies – such as radar – developed during the Second World War, which could be applied to accelerators. Also, after the war, the reputation of physicists was high because of their achievements and this meant governments were more willing to fund their research.

As well as a revolution in accelerator design, there were new, more efficient particle detectors. These came

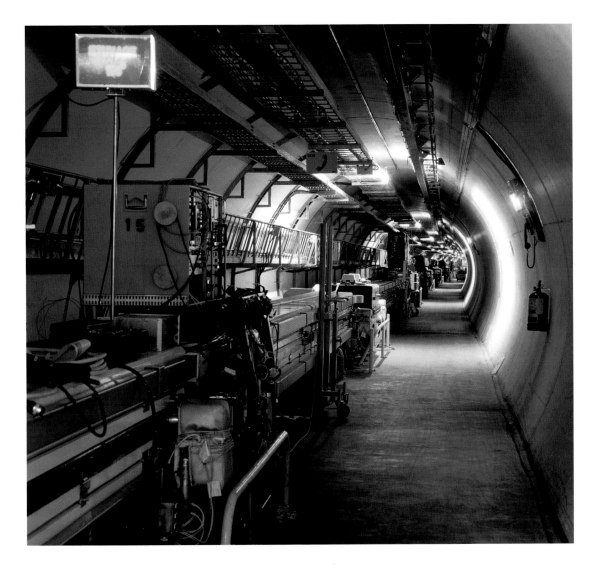

about more through necessity than anything else — there had to be more accurate ways to capture the results of experiments simply to keep up with the flood of data from the new machines.

One of these new machines was the bubble chamber. Bubble chambers are broadly based on the old-fashioned cloud chambers used before the war, but they use much more sophisticated technology. They consist of large refrigerated tanks of liquid hydrogen, which are placed as targets in a beam of particles from an accelerator. Some of the beam particles smash into the protons in the hydrogen nuclei. The electrically charged fragments from these

ABOVE: *This particle accelerator is at CERN, the European centre for particle physics near Geneva in Switzerland. The first particle accelerators were used in 1932 and it was this kind of machine that James Chadwick used to discover the missing neutron.*

Fact

THE BIG BANG

Accelerators like the ones at Fermilab and CERN probe the structure of matter in minuscule detail. In accelerator reactions, conditions begin to approach the extreme conditions that scientists believe existed soon after the Big Bang, the point at which the Universe was created. As well as providing information about the properties of particles, the experiments shed light on the development of the Universe in the tiny fractions of a second after the Big Bang.

ABOVE: Fermilab in Chicago. The figure-of-eight shape shows the two main particle accelerators, which have revealed information about atomic structure that would have been unbelievable only 50 years ago.

collisions pass through the liquid hydrogen. As they do so, they leave a trail of bubbles. These trails are photographed and later measured to give details of the particles involved in any interactions that have taken place. When bubble chambers were first used, the task of analysing the tracks was immense – tens of thousands of photographs had to be scanned. The invention of faster and more powerful computers meant that new kinds of electrical detectors could be built that selected specific particle 'events'. Information about these events could then be stored directly on a computer; this made it possible to analyse many more events and to look for rarer kinds of particle interactions.

Today, research on subatomic or particle physics is carried out in large international laboratories with huge accelerators, the bigger and more powerful descendents of the accelerators built in the 1930s. Two of the main centres are Fermilab in Chicago in the United States and CERN near Geneva in Switzerland. Large collaborations of scientists and engineers carry out research using state-of-the-art technologies in these laboratories.

BACK TO THE BUILDING BLOCKS

As scientists could study particle interactions in more and more detail, they noticed slight differences in their properties and behaviour. Could this profusion of particles be explained by having a small number of 'building blocks' that joined together in many different combinations? This had worked with chemical compounds. Fewer than 100 chemical elements are needed to make up all the chemicals in the Universe. Atoms have building blocks of protons, neutrons and electrons, which make up all the different atoms. We find ourselves back where we started – wondering if there is a truly 'fundamental' building block of matter.

QUARKS AND OTHER PARTICLES

Today most particle physicists agree that our Universe is made up of two groups of particles – quarks and leptons. Sticking the quarks together are other particles called gluons.

The theory of the quark was first suggested in 1964 by the US physicists Murray Gell-Mann and George Zweig. They both believed the quark was a building block of a proton or a neutron and was truly 'elementary', that is, it could not be divided. A few

BELOW: Electrons and neutrinos belong to the group of particles known today as leptons. This bubble-chamber photograph shows a neutrino interacting with an electron, then emerging as a neutrino again (the white track on the right-hand side).

years later, the massive particle accelerator in Stanford, California proved Gell-Mann and Zweig right. One surprising feature of this discovery was that quarks turned out to have fractional electric charges, 1/3 or 2/3 that of a proton. This means that a proton must be made up of three quarks. Electrons and neutrinos (the tiny particles created during nuclear reactions) are part of another group of 'elementary' particles – leptons.

Today these ideas form part of what we call the Standard Model. In this model, everything is explained by using six different quarks, which are matched by six leptons. The six quarks are called 'up', 'down', 'strange', 'charm', 'bottom', and 'top'. For example, a proton is a combination of two 'up' quarks and one 'down' quark, a neutron is a combination of one 'up' and two 'down' quarks. To go with these particles, there are four forces. The forces are gravity, electromagnetic, weak, and strong (the force that Werner Heisenberg had shown existed back in the 1930s). All this very complicated physics proves a valuable point – despite all the research scientists have done over the past 200 years, and all the great leaps they have made in explaining the structure of the atom, it is still not fully understood and may reveal even more secrets.

Key People

Murray Gell-Man (b. 1929) was an American physicist. He was exceptionally talented at science even as a child, and went to Yale University at the age of only 15. He was working at a time when many unidentified particles were being discovered – what we now call elementary particles. He was interested in understanding and classifying these new particles. He grouped together particles that shared similar properties and he even left gaps in his tables for particles he thought must exist but had not yet been found. Back in the nineteenth century, Dmitri Mendeleev had done the same thing when he put all the known elements into a table. Gell-Mann was awarded the Nobel Prize in 1969 for his many contributions to particle physics.

WHAT NEXT?

The path to splitting the atom was full of surprises, and the secrets the atom revealed were equally surprising. The programme of identifying 'building-blocks' of matter has been very fruitful. But information is still being discovered about these building blocks, and what goes on inside subatomic particles. Matter is made of atomic building blocks, atoms are made of protons, neutrons, and electrons. Protons and neutrons are made of quarks. And quarks? That is for you to find out.

BELOW: *A proton is made up of three quarks – two 'up' quarks (blue) and one 'down' quark (red).*

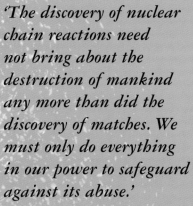

'*The discovery of nuclear chain reactions need not bring about the destruction of mankind any more than did the discovery of matches. We must only do everything in our power to safeguard against its abuse.*'

ALBERT EINSTEIN, 1953

TIMELINE

c. 400 BC	Democritus suggests that everything in the Universe is made up of tiny indivisible particles of matter
1789	Antoine Lavoisier draws up the first table of chemical elements
1803	John Dalton revives the atomic theory of matter
1815	William Prout suggests that atoms might be made up of even more fundamental 'building blocks', which he calls protyles
1869	Dmitri Mendeleev arranges the chemical elements into seven groups with similar properties, forming the basis of the periodic table
1895	Wilhelm Röntgen discovers X-rays
1896	Henri Becquerel discovers radioactivity in uranium
1897	J. J. Thomson discovers electrons
1898	Ernest Rutherford studies radiations from uranium and thorium and names them alpha and beta particles
1901	Marie Curie discovers polonium and radium
1905	Albert Einstein discovers the photoelectric effect
1911	Rutherford explains the results of the famous gold-foil experiment
1913	Henry Moseley's experiments with X-rays reveal information about atomic numbers and the positive charge of atoms
1919	Francis Aston discovers isotopes
1921	Rutherford suggests a third subatomic particle – the neutron
1922	Niels Bohr suggests a new 'planetary' model of the atom
1925	Patrick Blackett photographs a collision between an alpha particle and a nitrogen nucleus
1927	G. P. Thomson demonstrates the wave nature of the electron
1929	The Cockcroft-Walton accelerator is built
1930	Ernest Lawrence builds the cyclotron; Paul Dirac proposes the existence of antimatter and antiparticles
1932	James Chadwick discovers the neutron
1934	Enrico Fermi discovers the neutrino
1939	Nuclear fission is achieved
1942	Fermi conducts the first controlled nuclear chain reaction
1945	The USA drops the first two atomic bombs on the Japanese cities of Hiroshima and Nagasaki
1950	American scientists begin work on the hydrogen bomb
1956	The world's first full-scale nuclear reactor is completed in England
1964	Murray Gell-Mann suggests the existence of 'elementary' particles – quarks
2000	Evidence for a new elementary particle, the Higgs boson, is discovered at CERN

GLOSSARY

ACCELERATOR A large machine that accelerates beams of particles so they travel at high speeds, close to the speed of light.

ALPHA PARTICLE A particle emitted from the nucleus of an atom during radioactive decay, containing two protons and two neutrons.

ATOM The smallest unit that has the chemical properties of an element. Atoms are about a ten-billionth of a metre (10^{-10} m) in diameter.

ATOMIC BOMB Any nuclear weapon that uses fission to release energy; atomic bombs use either uranium or plutonium.

ATOMIC NUMBER The number of protons an element has in the nucleus of its atom.

BETA PARTICLE A particle emitted from an atom during radioactive decay. They can be either electrons or positrons.

CATHODE RAYS Streams of negatively charged electrons emitted from a negative electrode.

COSMIC RAYS High-energy subatomic particles, usually protons and helium nuclei, that travel through space at speeds close to the speed of light.

ELECTRODE An electrical conductor through which a current enters or leaves a medium.

ELECTROLYSIS The process by which compounds are broken down into their component elements by passing an electric current through water.

ELECTROMAGNETIC RADIATION Any form of radiation that uses electric and magnetic fields to move through space. This type of radiation can move through a vacuum.

ELECTRON An elementary particle and unit of negative electricity. Electrons are classed as one of a group of particles called leptons.

FISSION A process where the nucleus of a heavier element such as uranium splits into two chunks releasing a lot of energy while it does so.

FUSION A process where nuclei of light atoms such as hydrogen combine together to form a new element.

GAMMA RAYS A form of electromagnetic radiation, with very high energy and short wavelengths.

GLUON The particle that carries the 'strong interaction' force in an atom's nucleus. Gluons hold the quarks together.

GRAVITY The force acting between any two masses or bodies; the attraction that exists between two objects. Gravity is one of four forces scientists believe act even on subatomic particles.

HYDROGEN BOMB A bomb that uses nuclear fusion to release the energy that binds the nuclear particles together.

ISOTOPE An atom of the same element, but which has a different number of neutrons in the nucleus, and therefore a different mass.

KINETIC ENERGY The energy a body has because of its motion.

LEPTON A fundamental particle – electrons and neutrinos are leptons.

MASS A measure of how much matter something contains.

MATTER Anything that has a mass and takes up space.

MOLECULE A group of atoms that can exist on their own, held together by chemical bonds.

NEUTRINO A particle emitted during the process of nuclear fission. Neutrinos have no electric charge and very low mass.

NEUTRON A particle found in the nucleus with no electric charge. It is the counterpart to the proton.

NUCLEAR REACTOR A large machine in which a nuclear fission chain reaction is generated and controlled.

NUCLEUS The central core of an atom, about one thousand million-millionth of a metre (10^{-15} m) in diameter. It has a positive electric charge and is made of protons and neutrons. Electrons circulate around it.

ORBIT The region in which electrons move around the nucleus of an atom; also called shells.

PERIODIC TABLE The table of chemical elements, in which they are arranged across rows in order of increasing atomic number.

This means that elements with similar properties fall in the same column.

PHOTON The basic unit of light or other electromagnetic radiation. Atoms can emit or absorb energy in the form of photons.

PROTON A positively charged particle found in the nucleus of atoms. The number of protons in a nucleus fixes the chemical properties of an atom.

QUANTUM MECHANICS The study of physics on tiny scales, such as subatomic particles.

QUARK A particle that makes up protons and neutrons; the other group of these elementary particles is leptons. These particles affect each other through a range of forces.

RELATIVITY A collection of theories first suggested by Albert Einstein, which make several predictions about light, time, mass and motion, and which form the basis of our understanding of the Universe today.

STRONG INTERACTION The force that binds quarks together.

THERMAL ENERGY Energy in the form of heat.

VACUUM A region where there is no free matter. Space is a vacuum.

VOLT A unit of electrical energy.

X-RAYS A form of electromagnetic radiation with very short wavelengths and high energy.

FURTHER INFORMATION

WEB SITES

www.howstuffworks.com/atom.htm
This site covers many subjects, but includes detailed information about the structure of atoms, what they weigh, how atom smashers work, and much more.

www.public.web.cern.ch/Welcome.html
The home page for CERN, the world's largest particle physics laboratory.

www.lbl.gov/abc/
A good introduction to nuclear physics, with diagrams and definitions about everything from the basic structure of the atom to radioactivity and the cosmic connection.

BOOKS

Albert Einstein by Struan Reid: Groundbreakers, Heinemann Library, 2001
Atoms by Don Nardo: The Kidhaven Science Library, Kidhaven Press, 2001
Atoms and Elements by David Bradley and Ian Crofton: Oxford University Press, 2002
Atoms in Action by Susan Lakin: The Book Guild, 2003
Hiroshima: The Story of the First Atom Bomb by Clive A. Lawton: Franklin Watts, 2004
Ernest Rutherford and the Explosion of Atoms by John L. Heilbron: Oxford University Press, 2003

OTHER SOURCES

Scientists are discovering more about the atom all the time, as technology advances. Keep an eye out in newspapers and magazines, as well as watching the news on television, for all the latest developments.

INDEX